Winning Widows

Winning Widows

"A Study in the Book of Ruth"
with
Barbara J. White

Christian Literature & Artwork
A BOLD TRUTH Publication

Copyright

WINNING WIDOWS
Copyright © 2019 by Barbara J. White
ISBN 13: 978-1-949993-07-3

Healing For the Nations Ministries
PO Box 79126
Corona, California 92877-9998, USA
www.fmint.org ▪ *fmint2010@hotmail.com*

BOLD TRUTH PUBLISHING
(Christian Literature & Artwork)
606 West 41st, Ste. 4
Sand Springs, Oklahoma 74063
www.BoldTruthPublishing.com ▪ *beirep@yahoo.com*

Available from Amazon.com and other retail outlets. Orders by U.S. trade bookstores and wholesalers.

Quantity sales special discounts are available on quantity purchases by corporations, associations, and others. For details, contact the publisher at the address above.

Cover Art & Design by Aaron Jones

All rights reserved under International Copyright Law. All contents and/or cover art and design may not be reproduced in whole or in part in any form without the express written consent of the Author.

Printed in the USA.
07 19   10 9 8 7 6 5 4 3 2 1

Permissions

We would like to recognize and thank these Publiishers, for publishing and distributing the following versions of God's written Word.

> *The Lord gave the word: great was the company of those that published it.* - Psalm 68:11 (KJV)

Copyright 1995 by The Zondervan Corporation and the Lockman Foundation. Scripture marked AMP are taken from THE AMPLIFIED BIBLE, Old Testament Copyright © 1965, 1987, by the Zondervan Corporation. The Amplified New Testament Copyright, © 1958, 1987 by The Lockman Foundation. Used by permission.

"Scripture quotations taken from the Amplified® Bible *Classic Edition* (AMPC), Copyright © 1954, 1958, 1962, 1964, 1965, 1987 by The Lockman Foundation. Used by permission. www.Lockman.org"

Scripture quotations marked HCSB are taken from the Holman Christian Standard Bible®, Used by Permission HCSB © 1999, 2000, 2002, 2003, 2009 Holman Bible Publishers. Holman Christian Standard Bible®, Holman CSB®, and HCSB® are federally registered trademarks of Holman Bible Publishers.

Unless otherwise indicated, all Scripture quotations are taken from the KING JAMES VERSION (KJV): KING JAMES VERSION, public domain.

Permissions

"Scripture quotations marked NASB are taken from the New American Standard Bible®, Copyright © 1960, 1962, 1963, 1968, 1971, 1972, 1973, 1975, 1977, 1995 by The Lockman Foundation. Used by permission."

"Scripture quotations marked NIV are taken from the Holy Bible, New International Version®. NIV®. Copyright © 1973, 1978, 1984 by International Bible Society. Used by permission of Zondervan. All rights reserved."

Content

Foreword
The Widows are in Town! .... *i*

Chapter 1
Three Widows — Three Choices 1

Chapter 2
Two Widows Arrive in Bethlehem 11

Chapter 3
Naomi's Plan 17

Chapter 4
Widows, Godly Choices Are Vital to Your Future and Blessings 25

Chapter 5
Dwelling in The House of Bread 31

Chapter 6
Joy and Gladness 35

Chapter 7
God's Vision for Your Future 41

Foreword

Foreword
The Widows are in Town!

This book was birthed out of an experience I had in Mexicali, Mexico in August 2014, shortly after my husband was promoted to Heaven.

Five weeks after my husband, Gordon, went to be with the Lord, I had a phone call from Rachel Jeffries; a widow, and long-time close friend in ministry. We have known each other for over forty-one years. She shared with me that she would be in California ministering during the month of August.

"Would you like to go to Mexico with me on one of the weekends?" she asked.

I was a little stunned. My mind tried to provide a good reason for going. I wondered if it would be appropriate, since Gordon had so recently gone to Heaven. Religious thinking and traditions, can rob you of the blessings God has planned for you to bring healing and wholeness. Years ago, widows would hide away in

Foreword

their homes to grieve, wearing black clothes and believing they were respecting the life of their loved one. This only held them in grief and sadness, and their recovery was delayed; as a result.

Rachel stood with me in prayer during my husband's final months here on the earth, and encouraged me to walk through grief with victory and strength. I could call or text Rachel at any time and when I opened my heart to her, she was there to pray, walk with me in faith, and offer strong encouragement. She was a good listener and counselor; therefore, I gave attention to the *words of wisdom* she spoke into my life *by the Holy Spirit*. What I believed in my heart, was sustained by the sweet ministry of the Holy Spirit. Rachel's anointed words were very timely and helped me to maintain my vision for the future.

"I will pray about it and get back to you as soon as possible," I quickly replied to Rachel's loving request.

As soon as I got off the phone and prayed about whether to go or not, the Lord said, *"Go."* I knew God gave me the green light; because, my heart was filled with peace. I imagined Gordon saying to me in his sweet voice, *"Barbara, you go and enjoy yourself, and be a blessing to Rachel and the people in Mexico."* My mind settled down and I agreed with the Lord, knowing He

Foreword

had a wonderful purpose for this ministry trip to Mexico. I knew I was released to go by the Holy Spirit.

Even though, my emotions were fragile, and my physical body was in pain from the stress of caring for my husband, and my nervous system was compromised. Still, I made the choice to put my feelings and pain aside and allow *the joy of the Lord* to flow in me and out of me. This decision gave me supernatural strength, and a birthing took place for future ministry.

The purpose for this ministry trip: was to help and support Rachel. Then a most interesting thing happened after our arrival in Mexico, the Pastor, who drove us to Mexicali from Indio, California, spoke to me at our motel. He shared with me that he was going to tell the people in the church not to feel sorry for themselves. If they thought they had problems, they were to remember that two widows were there to minister to them. Rachel did not hear this conversation. As she was preparing to preach that evening, and still did not have a clear word on the topic she should minister. She had been waiting on the Lord for three weeks, for the right message to preach that evening. We both were praying for the meeting, knowing the Lord would give her the exact message for the people. It was now just two hours before the meeting!

Foreword

Sometime during our prayer time, I mentioned to Rachel the words the pastor spoke to me, and she immediately exclaimed, *"The Widows are in town!"* We laughed, cried, rejoiced, prayed, and continued to prepare ourselves for how the Lord wanted to use us. The Lord moved mightily in the meeting. Hungry hearts were blessed, and others were baptized in the Holy Spirit. Near the end, I had the privilege of praying with the believers through an interpreter.

While we were in Mexicali, we heard the news of a fire in a local orphanage, that was associated with the church. The children's mattresses had been burned and the metal bed frames charred. When we visited the home in the afternoon, the sweet children happily greeted us as we drove up, and quickly served us a drink as we sat fellowshipping in the yard. Rachel and I were so moved by the Holy Spirit to help in some practical way. Through tears, I said to Rachel, *"We need to help them purchase new mattresses."* We quickly responded to the need. The enemy tried to cause harm to the children, but God had protected them and now He was providing. Today, they have better facilities than they ever had before the fire.

The weekend in Mexico brought about a great healing in my emotions. I had chose to make a decision to follow the leading of the Holy Spirit, which brought me

Foreword

such relief from the pain of grief. So, instead of feeling sorry for myself, staying home, and allowing depression to envelope me; instead, I looked to Jesus and He led me so beautifully and comforted me as I was available to comfort others.

The restoration from grief had already begun, and was working in my spirit, penetrating its way into my deepest hurting soul, mind, and emotions. I not only knew it, but experienced God's mighty power. Thank God, His grace strengthened me to rise up in His power. He knew what I needed, and orchestrated the perfect plan for me to follow for my recovery. It was a big step of faith and the Lord honored His Word and did so much more than what I had asked or thought. *(cf. Eph. 3:20)*

The next day, we were in a church in Indio, California, and Rachel was the visiting speaker that afternoon. As the service progressed, a power point appeared with our photos and these words were projected on the screen—THE WIDOWS ARE IN TOWN! These words birthed the idea of Rachel writing a book on widows of the Bible. I too, felt I should write on this subject, and chose *the Book of Ruth*. I pray it will comfort and bless you.

Other ideas were birthed in me that weekend, one being a ministry page for widows on Facebook called:

Foreword

Winning Widows. The following year the Lord opened the way for me to minister to a group of widows in Bermuda.

As I began to journal how the Lord ministered to me on a daily basis, I was led to write a book to help others, whose loved one or friend had gone on to Heaven. This ministry trip to Mexico, played a part in giving me the vision to write my book, ***Navigating Through The Maze of Grief.***

Winning Widows

Chapter 1
Three Widows — Three Choices

I can imagine the young bride's thoughts were not on her work. In a few days she would become the wife of Elimelech, a wealthy young man who was well able to provide for her every need. Naomi's anticipated marriage to this handsome young man from Bethlehem-Judah; brought peace to her heart. Naomi loved Elimelech, and started day-dreaming of their life together. *How many children will the Lord bless us with? What is God's plan for us as we walk in the blessing of Abraham, the blessing of our covenant with Jehovah?*

We don't know how long Naomi and Elimelech had been married, but the Lord blessed them with two sons, Mahlon, meaning *sick*, and Chilion, whose name means *pining*. Whatever prompted them to name their children with such negative meanings is not understood. Naming your children in Bible times was important and most parents chose a name which expressed godly character.

Naomi was happy in her role as wife and mother. But

Winning Widows

suddenly, their circumstances were altered. A drought in the land of Israel, had brought about a famine. Lack of food caused Elimelech to allow fear to torment him and worry overwhelmed him when he thought about his family's needs. Fear was the root cause of his unwise decision to leave his homeland and move to the land of Moab. This heathen land, was known for its fertile plain. Moab may have had plenty of food, but Elimelech removed himself and his family from the land of blessing, exposing Naomi and their sons to the godless atmosphere of Moabites; they were given to idolatry. This heathen country held Israel in servitude [eighteen years] during the rule of the judges.

Elimilech: Did you not know the consequences of disobeying the commandments of the Lord, one may ask? He made a wrong choice, and as a result, ended up in a cursed nation outside the will of God for him and his family. Now, Satan is the author of disobedience, tormenting our minds and flesh with thoughts that God will not make His Word good in our lives. Elimilech's decision affected his wife and two sons and they suffered as a result of his selfish judgment.

Elimelech didn't live up to the meaning of his name, *God is King*. If he had remained and believed the promises of the Abrahamic Covenant, he would have proved that God truly is King. Regardless of the cir-

Winning Widows

cumstances, his every need would have been met; because, he was in covenant with the God of Israel. Long life, as well as freedom from sickness and disease was promised if the law was observed. Otherwise, a person's life was cut short if the law was not adhered to.

> *And ye shall serve your God, and he shall bless thy bread, and thy water; and I will take sickness away from the midst of thee.* – Exodus 23:25

The Lord repeated His promise of freedom from sickness and diseases in *Deuteronomy 7:15,*

> *And the Lord will take away from thee all sickness, and will put none of the evil diseases of Egypt, which thou knowest, upon thee; but will lay them upon all them that hate thee.*

During this time in history, Israel was ruled by judges, but we do not know which one was in power during this era. Israel was the land chosen by God for His people to dwell in, with the blessing of abundant provisions, as long as they followed the instructions of Jehovah. We don't know why the famine came or how long it lasted, but those who remained in their homeland survived the famine while others prospered.

The name Bethlehem means: *house of bread.* It is amaz-

Winning Widows

ing that Elimelech didn't understand that Jehovah would always provide bread (provision) for his family. It seems he chose to escape the trial, not willing to stay in faith and remain in his home town, nor even assist in alleviating the problem. His wealth could have been a blessing to many there.

~

If he had remained and believed the promises of the Abrahamic Covenant, he would have proved that God truly is King. Regardless of the circumstances his every need would have been met; because, he was in covenant with the God of Israel.

I am sure the decision to leave Bethlehem brought anxiety to Naomi's heart. In those days, a woman did not have an option and would follow her husband, even if his choice was made outside the will of God. However, she and their two sons followed Elimelech to a nation renowned for its idolatry and paganism. Moabites worshipped other gods, which included blood sacrifices, including child sacrifices to Molech. Elimelech did not prosper in the land of Moab, and before long he died, leaving Naomi a widow in a cursed, heathen land.

Winning Widows

Did Naomi live up to her name, meaning *my pleasant one*? She was sorely tested to remain loving and steadfast in the face of living in a strange land, and ultimate widowhood. Her financial resources were coming to a sad end.

Elimelech's decision to move Naomi and their sons from the land of promise and provision to the land of Moab, brought heartache to Naomi. Her sons married Moabite women. Mahlon married Ruth and Chilion married Orpah. I read that Orpah's ancestors included Goliath, the Philistine giant, which would make Orpah, Goliath's great grandmother; however, I cannot verify this. But as a Moabitess, she did not have a godly heritage. The name *Orpah* means: *hind, fawn, and stiff-necked*. The name *Ruth* means: *beauty*. Naomi had lost a husband and two sons, in the ten years they had dwelt in Moab.

I am certain Naomi told her daughters-in-law of her true God and the blessings bestowed upon her in her covenant with Jehovah. Otherwise, how could Ruth make such a bold faith confession to Naomi in *Ruth 1:16*?

> *And Ruth said, Entreat me not to leave thee, or to return from following after thee: for wither thou goest, I will go, and where thou lodgest, I will lodge: thy people shall be my people, and thy God my God.*

Winning Widows

Ruth made a bold decision with this confession, revealing her consecration to follow the God of Israel. Did she know her commitment would result in living and enjoying the rich rewards of the Abrahamic Covenant? She would soon experience the blessing of following Jehovah, far above and beyond what she could have imagined. Ruth grew up knowing nothing of the God of love and mercy; her gods were angry and needed to be appeased.

We don't know how long it was before Mahlon and Chilion died. We do know, three widows were left to grieve their losses. What were they to do? Naomi began processing her suffering and grief, but she had a yearning to return to her native land, Israel; where she knew the blessing rested. She heard that the Lord had *visited his people in giving them bread. (See: Ruth 1:6)*

Her memories of a blessed life in their Bethlehem home with her husband and sons, gave her hope that God would bring restoration to her sad losses. As a widow, she was now free to make her own decision in this matter. Naomi looked in faith beyond the hopelessness of her present situation, and seriously wondered when she should leave. It was a journey of over one hundred miles through rough terrain and mountains. Her financial resources were almost depleted, but she mustered up faith in Jehovah, knowing He would favor and protect her as

Winning Widows

she journeyed on foot. *"Maybe the Lord will provide a donkey along the way,"* she could have questioned in her heart, with a longing for this provision.

Naomi's love and concern for her daughters-in-law weighed on her heart. I read a fascinating quote from an unknown reference,

A famine in the fields of Bethlehem took Naomi to Moab; but now a famine in her heart, made her hunger after Bethlehem.

Naomi did not require Ruth and Orpah to return with her, as she could not guarantee there would be husbands to provide for the two young women in Bethlehem. In fact, she discouraged them from accompanying her,

> *And Naomi said, Turn again, my daughters: why will ye go with me? are there yet any more sons in my womb, that they may be your husband's?*
> *– Ruth 1:11*

Naomi also knew the prejudice that existed in Israel against the Moabites. Naomi's name, which means: *my pleasant one*, had an effect on the two widows, as they started to accompany her beginning the long journey homeward. *Ruth 1:8* reveals Naomi's love for her daughters-in law and their love for her, as she

Winning Widows

unselfishly tried to persuade them to stay with their families in their homeland,

> ...Go, each return to her mother's house: the Lord deal kindly with you, as ye have dealt with the dead, and with me.   – Ruth 1:8b

Naomi stopped and urged them to stay in their own land, and commended them for their kindness shown toward her sons. Then, Ruth and Orpah were affectionately kissed by their mother-in-law, weeping together on the dusty road in the heat of the day.

Naomi's grief overwhelmed her as she made a sad, misinformed statement: *The hand of the Lord is gone out against me.* (See: Ruth 1:13)

In her grief and sorrow, she was blaming God for her dilemma, as so many people do today. If she only had had a revelation of the nature of Father God, how He does not steal, kill, or destroy. Jesus came to Earth, revealing to us the nature of His Father—love, mercy, and grace. He is the giver of divine life *(cf. John 10:10)*. Naomi made the decision to return to the place where she had gone out of the will of God, even though she knew she was in a far worse condition than when she left.

The widows wept once more in anguish; Orpah kissed

Winning Widows

her mother-in-law for the last time and turned back to her mother's home. She was living up to her name—*stiffnecked*. On the other hand, Ruth clave to Naomi like one would cling to glue, and like a husband is to *cleave* to his wife *(cf. Genesis 2:24)*. Her heart was resolute and determined to follow a woman who imparted the knowledge of the true God of Israel to her heart. Ruth's name also means *friend* and she lived up to not only her name, but her character became that of a woman who served others with humility. She consecrated her life to serve Jehovah.

Ruth's unconditional and steadfast commitment to Naomi, as recorded in *Ruth 1:16 – 17* was her dedication to the God of Israel,

> *And Ruth said, Entreat me not to leave thee, or to return from following after thee: for wither thou goest, I will go; and where thou lodgest, I will lodge: thy people shall be my people, and thy God my God: Where thou diest, I will die, and there will I be buried: the Lord do so to me, and more also, if ought but death part thee and me.*

With a godly determination and commitment to Naomi, Ruth turned her back on her family and her heathen gods. No more was said, and the two widows started their long, weary, and dusty journey to Bethlehem.

Winning Widows

Winning Widows

Chapter 2
Two Widows Arrive in Bethlehem

All the people of Bethlehem were amazed, when they saw Naomi returning to her beloved city.

Oh, don't call me Naomi anymore; call me Mara (bitter). I went out full and the Lord has brought me home again empty. (See: Ruth 1:20 – 21a)

Her reasoning was based on widowhood and dire circumstances. Her bitterness toward God was expressed in these words; *Surely the Almighty has afflicted me (cf. Ruth 1:21).* She reveals the pain and anguish felt in her heart and soul, from losing a husband and two sons. Her emotions were severely wounded. Her widowhood was almost too much to bear. Naomi not only reflected on her pain, but she openly declared her sorrow and feelings to the people in the town.

At our lowest, God has not forgotten us, nor will He ever. He always desires to fulfill the wonderful plans He has purposed for us in love. God had not afflicted her; but He was setting her up for the restoration of the bless-

Winning Widows

ing; which belonged to her in the Abrahamic Covenant.

Naomi was greeted by the people of Bethlehem with the question: *"Is this Naomi?"* Her response was not what they expected.

Naomi sorrowfully declared: *Don't call me Naomi, call me Mara: for the Almighty hath dealt very bitterly with me. I went out full, and the Lord hath brought me home again empty: why then call ye me Naomi, seeing the Lord hath testified against me, and the Almighty hath afflicted me? (See: Ruth 1:20 – 21)*

Naomi was indeed *bitter* as the name Mara means. Her use of the word *Almighty* in blaming God for her dilemma, shows she had forgotten how good God is. He is El Shaddai, the All-Bountiful One, the All Sufficient One, who nourishes, satisfies, protects and supplies. Her grief and adverse circumstances clouded her thoughts temporarily, as to the absolute nature and goodness of God. All of Naomi's accusations against the Almighty One were unfounded. The word *afflicted* here does not mean bodily sickness and disease, rather it means *poverty-stricken*.

When we cling to the blessings of God and our covenant, there is always grace and restoration from God, even if mistakes were made, as in the case of Naomi's

Winning Widows

husband Elimelech, when he made that fateful decision to leave Judah. Naomi could have felt she was a victim, [and quite possibly she did], which was reflected in her negative confessions to the people of Bethlehem.

~

At our lowest, God has not forgotten us, nor will HE ever. He always desires to fulfill the wonderful plans He has planned in love for us.

The shame of widowhood, was visibly seen on Naomi's face. Aging lines revealed the care and worry brought about by her suffering and the enormous stress from the long journey home. The shame of having to look to others to provide for her, weighed heavily on her heart. She knew her finances were depleted; furthermore, there was no husband to support her and Ruth.

The time had come for each widow to shake the dust off her feet; symbolic of shaking off the hurt, reproach, offenses, pain from the past, and embracing the new life and blessings awaiting them. Naomi and Ruth did not have the *Book of Isaiah* to reference for comfort as we do:

> *Fear not, for thou shalt not be ashamed; neither be thou confounded; for thou shalt not be put*

Winning Widows

to shame; for thou shalt forget the shame of thy youth, and shalt not remember the reproach of thy widowhood anymore. – Isaiah 54:4

We have this Word from our Father God! We have a complete Bible, filled with great and precious provisions. These belong to us now and each day of our future with Him.

According as his divine power hath given unto us all things that pertain unto life and godliness, through the knowledge of him that hath called us to glory and virtue: Whereby are given unto us exceeding great and precious promises: that by these ye might be partakers of the divine nature, having escaped the corruption that is in the world through lust. – 2 Peter 1:3 – 4

Widows: never lose your hope in the God of all hope and comfort.

Now may the God of hope fill you with all joy and peace as you believe in him, so that you may abound in hope by the power of the Holy Spirit. – Romans 15:13

Keep an expectant and joyful attitude all along your journey to healing and wholeness.

Winning Widows

Godly faith and obedience, will always bring restoration and provision.

The widows returned to Bethlehem at the time of the barley harvest. Godly restoration brings provision and it was no coincidence—the timing was perfect on God's calendar. The widows positioned themselves to be in the right place at the right time.

I wonder what Ruth's first impressions were of her new home land? I am sure the little town of Bethlehem situated in the picturesque Judean Mountains, brought hope to the pain of loss. Ruth's confession of faith had aligned her with the God of Israel; she was about to see how good God is. Ruth's courageous choice to follow her mother-in-law back to Bethlehem released her from the idolatry and darkness of Moab, and brought her into the light of her new found God, Jehovah, and His Kingdom of blessing.

Even though Naomi was presently in a bitter state, Ruth clung to her hope in the God of Israel; thus releasing expectations of better days.

When we cling to the blessings of God and our covenant, there is always grace and restoration from God, even if mistakes were made.

Winning Widows

The Promised Land is where the provisions are to be found and enjoyed. Today, as believers, we are living in the promised Kingdom of God, [a land] filled with the full blessings and provisions Jesus purchased for us, to be received by faith in the finished work of Jesus.

Again, when Naomi and Ruth arrived in Bethlehem, they found that those who remained there during the famine had not only survived, but they had prospered. *(See: p. 3)* Some families had become wealthy as in the case of Boaz. A famine cannot stop the blessings of the Abrahamic Covenant.

Many natural concerns can be overwhelming. Opportunities can abound for a widow to succumb to fear and worry, like: *Where do my provisions come from, now that I am a widow?*

Winning Widows

Chapter 3
Naomi's Plan

God always has a good and perfect plan for His people. In times of trouble and despair, we need to hear and know in our heart—the specific plan He has for our deliverance.

Naomi knew there was a wealthy landowner in the city, Boaz by name. He was connected to her late husband, Elimelech. She was acquainted with the law of kinsman redemption, meaning that Ruth could qualify to be the wife of Boaz. One problem existed though; there was another kinsman who must relinquish his right to marry Ruth.

Ruth was accustomed to work, so she initiated a plan to go to the fields and join the poor who daily gathered their food, by gleaning the remnant of barley grain that was left on purpose by the reapers for the poor. She made a decision to busy herself and go to the fields to gather grain, asking permission from her mother-in-law. Ruth's suggestion was agreed to by Naomi, and she declared she would find grace while working in

Winning Widows

the field where she chose to glean. She believed Ruth would find favor with the owner of the barley field.

It was a humbling position, but Ruth was willing to take her place and be used to help provide for Naomi and herself. She stayed busy with the others, and gathered enough grain each day to meet the needs of both widows. I can imagine she joyfully sang, as she continued her daily labor, beginning in the cool of early morning hours, through the heat of the day, until it was time to return home. Ruth's loving character displayed an uncompromising faithful spirit, she was concerned for her mother-in-law's necessary daily provisions.

Ruth happened to end up in Boaz's field—but it wasn't a coincidence! Boaz, the prominent wealthy business man of Bethlehem, noticed Ruth, and gave her permission to glean in his field, warning the young men not to touch her or prevent Ruth from gleaning. Boaz asked his servant, *"Who is this damsel?"* Upon knowing who she was, he extended favor to Ruth, requesting she did not go to another field, but to abide in his. He afforded her protection from the men in the field, and water to refresh herself, that the young men had drawn. Furthermore, he instructed his workmen to drop barley on purpose so Ruth would have a more bountiful harvest to take home to Naomi. When Boaz extended his generosity to Ruth, he told her not to leave his field.

Winning Widows

Ruth was overcome with gratitude, and bowed herself to the master of the field, her awe-inspiring thoughts verbalized these words:

Then she fell on her face, bowing to the ground and said to him, Why have I found favor in your sight that you should take notice of me, since I am a foreigner? – Ruth 2:10 NASB

We see a sweet romance developing! We don't know exactly Ruth's physical beauty, but some writers and artists, have speculated that she had dark red hair with dark Middle Eastern eyes to match her olive skin. More importantly, she displayed a sweetness and humility that arrested Boaz's attention.

Boaz released a blessing to Ruth saying,
And now my daughter, do not fear. I will do for you whatever you ask, for all my people know that you are a woman of excellence. – Ruth 3:11 NASB

Boaz had been told of her loving care toward Naomi, and her willingness to leave her family and homeland. The words spoken by Boaz over Ruth that day were prophetic, releasing her to walk in the blessings of the God of Israel. Boaz knew Ruth had come to love Jehovah, the true God. The fruit in her life, revealed her genuine, loving heart. Boaz released a covenant blessing over this beautiful woman; it became her covering and protection.

> *May the Lord reward your work, and your wages be full from the Lord, the God of Israel, under whose wings you have come to seek refuge.*
> *– Ruth 2:12 NASB*

God had a beautiful plan for Ruth, a plan to bring a woman of Moab, a cursed race, into the commonwealth of Israel. The second blessing for Ruth, was being included in the genealogy of Jesus through her son Obed and King David. We were all aliens from the commonwealth of Israel and strangers from the covenants of promise, having no hope, and without God in this world. *(See: Ephesians 2:12)* God brought us into a covenant relationship with Him through the Blood of the Lord Jesus Christ *(cf. Ephesians 2:13)*.

God always has a good and perfect plan for His people.

Father God has full rewards for those who trust Him with all their heart. A complete trust in His faithfulness and goodness releases the widow from the grief and sorrow of loss. There is a new day dawning, the

Winning Widows

brilliant sunshine of God's favor is available and will grow stronger day by day. The blessings must be received in faith and with great joy.

Bereavement is destined to last only for a season. It must be processed day by day in the comfort, strength, and power of the Holy Spirit. A new life and a new season will come forth. Believers, cling to your Blood Covenant. Make faith withdrawals from every resource God has provided for you in Jesus.

It was time for the threshing of the grain. For it must be separated from the chaff to complete the harvest. The winnowing process took place in the cool of the night when the winds come up and the chaff is blown away, leaving the barley grain on the threshing floor.

Naomi knew Boaz would be at the threshing floor, and set forth to devise a plan. Her directions for Ruth began by instructing her to prepare herself by bathing, anointing herself with oil, (perfume) and dressing in her best garment. Naomi coached Ruth,

> *Wash yourself therefore, and anoint yourself and put on your best clothes, and go down to the threshing floor; but do not make yourself known to the man until he has finished eating and drinking. And it shall be when he lies down, that you*

Winning Widows

shall notice the place where he lies, and you shall go and uncover his feet and lie down; then he will tell you what you shall do. – Ruth 3:3 – 4 NASB

It probably seemed a strange request, but Ruth displayed a trust in Naomi and followed exactly the instructions of her mother-in-law. Startled at midnight Boaz realized it was Ruth who lay at his feet. He knew exactly why she was there, according to kinsman redeemer custom. In fact, he could have acted sooner in claiming her as his wife. Boaz commended Ruth for her humble and virtuous life. She had proved her godly character and he blessed her saying,

And now my daughter, fear not; I will do to thee all that thou requirest: for all the city of my people doth know that thou art a virtuous woman.
– Ruth 3:11

One problem remained to be resolved; there was a nearer kinsman who had first choice in claiming Ruth as his wife. The estate of Naomi's deceased husband Elimelech, must be redeemed. Boaz quickly went the next day to settle the matter with the elders at the gate of the city. With the required ten witnesses, the business of redemption proceeded, and the next of kin was told that if he redeemed the land belonging to Elimelech, a young widow called Ruth was included, and he

Winning Widows

must marry her and raise up seed to Elimelech.

I cannot redeem it, it will affect my inheritance, [was his response]. — *Ruth 4:5 – 6*

The ceremony proceeded according to Jewish custom, with the removal of a shoe passed to Boaz in the presence of the witnesses, sealing the transaction. The property now legally belonged to Boaz, and he could proceed with his marriage to his striking bride, Ruth. She fully cooperated and responded to the opportunity presented to her. Ruth saw the love Boaz had for her and beyond that, the love of God in him did not condemn her, put her down, or make her feel unworthy of his love.

In one day, Ruth went from being a forsaken Moabite and a poor widow, to becoming the wife of a wealthy man who loved and cared for her every need, and desire. This sounds like Jesus Who loved us, accepted us, redeemed us, and made us His very own.

What a beautiful fulfillment of God's favor and blessings upon Ruth. Her marriage to Boaz, released the blessing of the Abrahamic Covenant to Ruth and the blessing was restored to Naomi's life as well. Both women were no longer destitute and poor. God's restoration, in every sense of the word, was manifested in

Winning Widows

the lives of two desperate widows.

The greatest plan of Father God was realized and would affect every generation and person on Earth.

∽

There is a new day dawning and the brilliant sunshine of God's favor is available and will grow stronger day by day. The blessings must be received in faith and with great joy.

Winning Widows

Chapter 4
Widows, Choices Are Vital To Your Future and Blessings

We looked at the background of Orpah and her staunch religious commitment to the heathen Moabite religion. Apparently, her late Jewish husband did not convince her to serve the one true God, Jehovah. In her time of grief and overwhelming sadness she made a weak effort to follow her mother-in-law back to Judah. She was not convinced that this would be the best choice, so while on the road to Bethlehem she made her final decision and returned to her family. We read no further of her whereabouts or if she ever embraced Israel's God.

Naomi's spiritual foundation was solid, having been taught the law of the old covenant with its promises of a future Messiah-Redeemer. Her heart was so distressed when her husband moved her to the land of the heathen Moabites. I am sure she dreamed of the time when she could return home to the land of blessing with her husband. Yet, it was not to be, God was

Winning Widows

completely faithful in leading her back to the land of her birth—at the right season.

The disgrace of widowhood and poverty, weighed heavily on her heart, and the embarrassment of her desperate circumstances; was hard to bear. Her story reveals a woman who had strength of character and a strong will to seek God, no matter the cost or humiliation she was experiencing. The established heart is stable and fixed, not moved by adverse circumstances.

In *Psalms 112* we are told of the faith of the one who believes God's Word,

> *He will not fear evil tidings; His heart is steadfast, trusting in the Lord. His heart is upheld, he will not fear, until he looks with satisfaction on his adversaries.   – Psalm 112:7 – 8 NASB*

The choice Naomi made to return to the land of blessing, took her out of despair and set her on the path of restoration in every way. Her seed was birthed, and what a joy this grandson *(Obed)* brought to her life; he was a restorer in every sense of the word. The women of the town rejoiced with her.

> *Then the women said to Naomi, Blessed is the Lord who has not left you without a redeemer to-*

Winning Widows

day, and may his name become famous in Israel.
– Ruth 4:14 NASB

They went on to declare how Obed would be a nourisher and restorer of life, even a support in Naomi's old age. The blessing her daughter-in-law Ruth brought her, was a deep love that evidenced itself in every way.

The choices Naomi made brought rich rewards and joy to her aging life. The day her grandson Obed was born to Boaz and Ruth, was a highlight in her widowed state. She now had posterity with a family to love and cherish. And she had a part in training Obed in the Word of God.

∾

The established heart is stable and fixed, not moved by adverse circumstances.

Ruth's road to victory, began the day she committed to, not only follow her mother-in-law Naomi, but made the decision in her heart to honor and worship Jehovah. This victory was evidenced by her faith decision and corresponding action. Not knowing her future in Bethlehem, she set out to embrace a new life, no matter what the cost or change that would be required of her. Ruth must have wondered if her life and circumstances

Winning Widows

would ever improve. How could she rise out of poverty? Would she remarry and be happy? Would her desire to have a child come to pass? Many questions must have filled her heart and mind.

A deep love for Naomi was evidenced by Ruth, as she followed her instructions in every detail. She may not have understood Jewish traditions, but being a quick learner, enabled her to move forward in God's direction. *Obedience* to the leading of the Holy Spirit brought multiple blessings. God completely changed her life and her circumstances.

The blessing of the Abrahamic Covenant brought her into the land of plenty: as a result, she was no longer a poor and forsaken widow. I am sure at the beginning of her relocation to Bethlehem, Ruth did not fully comprehend God's ultimate plan and choice of a husband, or that she would be an important person in the fulfillment of the Seed of Abraham coming to Earth; to be mankind's Redeemer.

Ruth' son, Obed, was the grandfather of King David, making him a direct descendent of our wonderful Lord Jesus Christ. Ruth, the Moabitess, was adopted and accepted into God's magnificent plan, just as we have been accepted into the family of God. Once we were in darkness, but now we walk in the light and

Winning Widows

enjoy all the provisions of Kingdom living.

Boaz, Ruth's kinsman redeemer, is a picture of our Great Redeemer, the Lord Jesus Christ. What Boaz did for Ruth, Jesus did far above and beyond for us.

Winning Widows

Winning Widows

Chapter 5
Dwelling in the House of Bread

We don't know if Ruth understood the meaning of the name of her new dwelling place, when she first arrived in her new home. Bethlehem means: *house of bread*. When she entered the city limits, she entered into the place where unlimited provisions were available to her. The provisions and the blessings of the Abrahamic Covenant were now available for her—as a result of receiving the God of Abraham, and forsaking her heathen upbringing.

The *house of bread* meant the provisions were great and abundant. Naomi made the decision to return to her place of overflowing provisions. Ruth followed in her mother-in-law's footsteps, making a life-changing decision, that affected all her descendants.

Ruth stepped into the rich covenant blessings through God's abundant grace and mercy. She didn't earn it, and until the time she made the decision to follow the God of Naomi, she was outside the covenant promises. One decision made from her heart, changed her

Winning Widows

forever. In the same way, our decisions affect our life.

The *house of bread* is your divine *"dwelling place."* You [now] have a choice—live in the blessing or live in the curse.

Jesus Sets Us in a Large Place

I called upon the Lord in distress: the Lord answered me, and set me in a large place. The Lord is on my side; I will not fear: what can man do unto me? – Psalm 118:5 – 6

Although I wrote this book with widows in mind, this message applies to us all. The death, burial, and resurrection of the Lord Jesus Christ made THE WAY for us to enjoy our large place in Him.

The distressing circumstances a widow can find herself in after the death of her husband can be overwhelming. Grief brings sorrow and distress, which are often hard to bear and overcome.

The wonderful news is: Jesus has provided THE WAY out of all of these struggles. I pray the Scripture above speaks to your heart today, as it does to mine. The Lord is waiting for us to call upon Him in our distress. It is a cry made in faith, knowing that the Lord is good and

Winning Widows

His mercies endure forever. Never give up, speak to the Lord right in the middle of your pain and emotional upheaval. *He is a very present help in time of trouble,* including grief and sorrow. Today, draw from and receive His sweet comfort, knowing the *large place* is your place of wholeness and healing, with every provision available for you in Him.

∼

Naomi made the decision to return to her place of overflowing provisions.

Now this is the exciting part of this Scripture—*the Lord answered me.* Yes, He answers the heartfelt cry of His children. The answer came with this precious and wonderful provision—*He set me in a large place!* This is true freedom; including, no longer limited by restrictions of circumstances and pain. Completely free to enjoy the fullness of the blessing of healing, and the joy of the Lord.

Some translations use the words *broad* and *spacious* for the word *large*. This really paints the picture for us. This glorious provision, was paid for by Jesus on the cross with *His precious blood.* Just think about it, we don't have to struggle to get God to bring us into this LARGE PLACE of provisions and victory. It is

Winning Widows

there waiting for us to receive. It is up to us to take advantage of this freedom and wholeness provided for us through faith in—the blood of Jesus and the Word of God.

Winning Widows

Chapter 6
Joy and Gladness

Gladness and joy will overtake them and sorrow and sighing will flee away... – Isaiah 51:11a NIV

And the redeemed of the Lord shall return and come to Zion with singing, crowned with unending joy. Joy and gladness will overtake them, and sorrow and sighing will flee. – Isaiah 51:11 HCSB

We are called by God, *the redeemed of the Lord*. This revealed truth makes my heart glad. I want to shout for joy, just knowing by experience, the transforming life and nature of God; is alive in my spirit.

As a result of the new birth, we have obtained everlasting gladness and joy—supernatural forces in our spirit, to be released through our words and songs of praise.

The enemy's strategy is aimed to steal our joy through adverse circumstances, but, he can't take our joy; it dwells eternally in our spirit. The aim of the enemy,

Winning Widows

is to get you to stop praising and worshiping the Lord and speaking God's Word. Then your level of joy and strength dissipates, leaving you weak and ineffective.

Sighing is an expression of mourning, which can be expressed with groaning. It means: to often let out one's breath audibly, as a result of sorrow and weariness.

The answer to depression, sorrow, sighing, and mourning, is to make a quality decision to maintain a joyful heart. God Himself said, sorrow would flee away! If you will endeavor to faithfully praise and worship the Lord, releasing the joy in your spirit, the sadness and sorrow will leave. Singing and praising God, is the best reliever of sighing and sorrow. It is not something you do one time, it is a habit to be developed, a lifestyle to embrace. Take your place of aggressive persistence in the area of praise and worship.

Your spirit was created to house the nature of God, including joy and gladness. Joy and depression can't dwell together, they do not harmonize. We choose what takes precedence in our heart. Choose joy and gladness!

I pray today you will rise up in the power of the Holy Spirit, and release what God has placed in your spirit—joy and gladness. These traits will overtake you, and sorrow and sighing will flee!

Winning Widows

Make a quality decision not to be overtaken with sorrow and mourning; because, it will come, and you will be tempted to submit to it, but you can rise up, and release the supernatural joy in your spirit. That is when the darkness fleeing away takes place!

> *Thou has turned for me my mourning into dancing: thou hast put off my sackcloth, and girded me with gladness. To the end that my glory (tongue) may sing praises to thee, and not be silent, O Lord my God, I will give thanks unto thee forever.*
> – Psalm 30:11

Gladness belongs to the child of God! Joy unspeakable and full of God's glory, is in your spirit waiting to be released. Mourning will flee, sadness must go, at the sound of your praise and singing.

We are called to live in the light of God's love, free from all fear and sadness.

So take a step of faith today, and raise your voice in praise and singing. Sadness will flee and you will be tempted to dance with joy!

The God of All Grace

Recently, the Lord brought a Word to me to share

Winning Widows

with you. I pray for you and believe the Holy Spirit is strengthening you, spirit, soul, and body, especially in the emotional realm.

I kept hearing the words *"the God of all grace"* and when I checked it out in my Bible, I knew why God wanted me to share this with you.

> *But the God of all grace, who hath called us unto his eternal glory by Jesus Christ, after that ye have suffered awhile, make you perfect, stablish, strengthened, settle you.*   – 1 Peter 5:10

When Peter wrote this letter, he was sending encouragement to the believers who were dealing with much persecution. *Persecution* means suffering in our soulish realm, and often in the physical as well.

The good news is: We serve *the God of all grace*. He has made the way for us to live in the glory realm, otherwise He would not have called us there. It has been made possible by the Lord Jesus Christ. The glory is the manifested presence of God.

The last part of the verse talks about suffering. Let's apply this to the pain of sighing and grief. It is very real, and needs to be walked through and overcome by the blood of Jesus and the word of our testimony,

Winning Widows

which is the Word of God. *(See: Revelation 12:11)* Peter uses the word *awhile* meaning: it is not forever or ongoing! The grief in no way strengthens you; in fact, it can drain and weaken your spirit, your soul (mind and emotions), and your body.

~

If you will endeavor to faithfully praise and worship the Lord, releasing the joy in your spirit, the sadness and sorrow will leave. Singing and praising God is the best reliever of sighing and sorrow.

You see, the God of all grace imparts blessing and favor *(cf. 1 Peter 5:10 Amplified)*. They are present to perfect, establish, strengthen, and settle you. He strengthens us when we feel our heart is ripped apart by loss. Jesus Himself establishes and makes us what we ought to be and grounds us in Him. We are complete in Him *(Colossians 2:10)*. Praise God for this wonderful Word from the Father of all grace! I feel encouraged and strengthened myself just writing to you, sharing this anointed Word given to us by the Holy Spirit through our brother Peter.

Winning Widows

Rise up believers! Rise up and see yourself seated together with Jesus in the heavenly realm, reigning as an overcomer in this life.

Winning Widows

Chapter 7
God's Vision for Your Future

It is not unusual if your vision for the next phase of your life seems blurry for awhile after the death of a loved one. Your thoughts can be fuzzy for a time, while processing emotions of sadness and grief. There are many decisions to be made that are life-changing. Each one needs to be made by seeking God in prayer. It is imperative that your heart is attentive to hearing His Voice, then making notes of what He reveals.

Personally, I took it slow after my husband went on to be with the Lord. I chose not to be pressured or rushed into making decisions or changes in my life. I carefully sought the Lord, and by faith entered into His peace. It was not always easy, as sad or negative feelings and loneliness would try to overwhelm me. But I knew in my heart, it was the healthy way to proceed.

I knew with a God-given confidence it was right to keep doing, what I had been doing before my loss. I endeavored daily to keep a to-do-list, and that helped me stay focused on the tasks of life. To hide away and

Winning Widows

seldom communicate with family and friends can be devastating, it leads to depression and self-pity. Each day I purposed in my heart to communicate with family or friends, go outside my home, even just for a walk, or to go shopping. *Loneliness is a tool of the enemy* to hold you down, causing a depressed feeling. We are not called to live a solitary life in isolation, without companionship. Your family, friends, and your Church family are invaluable in supporting you in your walk of victory. Choose wisely who you associate with, confide in or allow into your life. Stay close to those that lift you up with encouraging words and prayer.

As you move forward in your healing and restoration toward wholeness in your emotions, clarity of thought will come. This transpires as a result of meditating and speaking God's Word on a daily basis. Your mind will respond to the Word you speak and think upon. The Lord longs to make Himself real to you in every area of your life. He will speak to you from His Word, and the Holy Spirit will quicken to your spirit, Words that give peace and direction. There is nothing more soothing to your soul, than to hear the sweet comforting Words the Holy Spirit speaks so gently to you. These Words are precious and should be held close to your heart. They minister healing to every hurting part of your being. The Holy Spirit ministers to us in a very personal way and He knows our deepest thoughts and

Winning Widows

longings of our soul. Take time to journal all the precious Words the Holy Spirit speaks to you.

Our New Covenant is established on better promises, signed and sealed with the blood of Jesus. God still gives vision and hope to His people, just like He did for Naomi and Ruth. So, ask the Lord what He wants you to do. He will show you and it will be good and perfect, filled with Words that cause joyful expectation and gladness in your spirit and soul. Then your body will respond as if you had taken a big dose of vitamins.

His Word will give you hope to plan for your future. Yes, you do have a future! When you hear the Voice of the Lord, your heart will be joyful and happy. It may take time for things to fall into place, but you can be sure that each move you make in faith—will be a step forward. Never think about returning back to how things were; for, they will never be the same. But that doesn't mean your *now season* and future will be any less blessed and fulfilling. In fact, I am convinced, your days ahead are destined to be filled with more glory, blessings, and the manifested presence of the Lord.

I personally found great comfort remembering the call of God on my life at the age of twelve. I knew the home going of my husband, did not alter God's plan for my life. I clung to what God spoke to me many years ago,

Winning Widows

and decided I was going to follow Him, trusting His great precious plan. To remain in God's perfect will was my top priority. We had ministered beautifully together as a husband and wife team for fifty years. Now I was alone, and I knew it was my responsibility to pursue God, to find out exactly how and when to proceed. There was no pressure—I did not give myself a timeline, but I moved forward with patience and a steadiness; only the Holy Spirit could impart to me. It was well worth waiting on the Lord in this matter.

We are not called to live a solitary life in isolation, without companionship. Your family, friends, and your Church family are invaluable in supporting you in your walk of victory.

It is important to cherish every precious memory you shared with your loved one. Look through photo albums and remember all the good times you spent together. *Journaling* is one way to record special events. I had recorded many of our ministry events in the nations, and had a multitude of photos as well. It brought great joy to my heart and thanksgiving, for all God had done in and through us during that time.

Winning Widows

I'd like to share with you an analogy I recently read; and it so aptly applies to this subject. I am borrowing the concept from someone else's writing and applying it to your individual situation. It totally blessed me, and I know you will be edified too. *We can look through a mirror or we can look through a window.* To look in a mirror we see ourselves in our present state. The image we see of ourselves can be devastating and hopeless, especially, if we are still processing grief and our emotions remain fragile. When you see yourself only in your present state, it gives no hope for your future.

On the other hand, when we look through a window, we see potential and a future. It's like looking at the precious provisions God has already provided for us in His Word. The Word of God always gives us hope and a vision for our future days. As the Word is *anointed,* the Holy Spirit comes to our aid, helping us to view our circumstances as God sees them. We are empowered by God to see beyond the image in the mirror.

Lack of hope robs you of the joyful expectation that God has revealed to you in His Word, and what has been imparted into your spirit. Your mind has a choice: What do I believe? What I see in the mirror, or what I perceive by the Holy Spirit through the window of the Word of God?

Winning Widows

While we look not at the things which are seen, but at the things which are not seen; for the things which are seen are temporal; but the things which are not seen are eternal. – 2 Corinthians 4:18

When we focus and concentrate on the things which we see in our mirror, we can become quickly discouraged. The devil may whisper, *"Nothing is going to change, you will always live in hopelessness, there is no future for you as a widow."*

Looking in your mirror is not wrong, just don't stay there, neither deny your present circumstances. We acknowledge the natural realm, and then move on in faith with a heart that is fully persuaded that circumstances and feelings are temporal, and subject to change. How? While we look not at the things which are seen, but at the unseen realm in the spirit—the Word of God!

As you look through your personal window of God-given opportunities for your future, your *vista* can be quite exhilarating. Any Words the Lord quickens to your heart, will cause hope to arise for your future, and faith to come alive for the *now season*. Your vision for the next day, week, month, or even longer, will become more clear, as you meditate on God's personal Words to you.

Winning Widows

Regrets

Don't be surprised if regrets bombard your mind. Emotions, if not harnessed, especially in the area of regrets, will hold you back in your walk toward healing, victory and wholeness.

Some of the accusations the enemy will bring to your mind will sound something like this: *"If only I had spent more time with my loved one"* or, *"Why didn't I ...?"* We open ourselves up to relive the failures of the past, accompanied by tormenting thoughts. It is a strategy of the enemy that needs to be quickly recognized and dealt with. We do not know everything, nor do we need to know. So, commit every past regret and question to the Lord, and walk free. It's a faith decision, that will guide you along the path of victory. It may seem like baby steps at first, but know you are making progress with your wonderful Helper, the Holy Spirit.

I can well imagine the regrets Naomi dealt with, when she went out of the will of God to a heathen nation. But she came to herself after the loss of her husband and two sons, and made a quality decision to return to the land of blessing. God was on her side, leading her every step of the way to recovery and restoration.

Winning Widows

We have been called into liberty as sons and daughters of the Most High God. His Word always brings liberty. This is our calling, to walk in godly freedom, and avoid at all costs being entangled with any yoke of bondage.

> *Stand fast therefore in the liberty wherewith Christ hath made us free, and be not entangled again with the yoke of bondage.* – Galatians 5:1

It takes a bold decision, with the help of the Holy Spirit, to rise up and let the regrets go, releasing them with words of faith out of your mouth. God is bigger than all your regrets!

Turning Disappointments into God's Appointments

I was particularly disappointed when my husband went to be with the Lord. It is the most natural thing to plan for your future, no matter how long you have been married or in ministry. During the last year my husband was here, I saw signs that indicated he would be going to Heaven. At first I didn't want to acknowledge it. The pain of loss, seemed too tough to bear, even before the departure of my loved one.

Finally, I accepted the reality of the circumstances and told the Lord I would release my husband to go home

Winning Widows

to be with Him. As a result, the comfort I received was supernatural. The Holy Spirit within, ministered great strength to me from day to day. I told my husband what God had shown me; I knew he was faithful to his calling, and he had fought a good fight of faith and finished his course. He went out of this life in faith and victory. I didn't need to understand everything, but to trust God with all my heart for the present and the future.

~

**So, commit every past regret and question to the Lord, and walk free.
It is a faith decision that will guide you along the path of victory.**

There are spiritual forces provided for us in God's Word that must be applied, to overcome disappointments. Disappointments are not your destination, it's a place that you are passing through. You may ask: *"How do I pass through this difficult season in my life?"*

Disappointments can hold power over you, if you do not know how to proceed and deal with it effectively. We have been given powerful spiritual weapons by our loving Heavenly Father, to move forward in grace and authority. To try and accomplish this with your mind and worldly wisdom, will leave you helpless and re-

Winning Widows

maining in the grip of despair and hopelessness.

Joy and peace are both supernatural fruits abiding in your recreated spirit; through the power of the Holy Spirit. These forces are part of your love-walk. *God is love,* and He has provided the way for you to live on a higher plane. These spiritual forces are not there for you to just feel good, they are mighty weapons to employ in times of trials and disappointments. When you read the *Book of Philippians*, Paul told the believers about thirteen times to rejoice in the Lord!

> *Rejoice in the Lord always; and again I say, Rejoice.* – Philippians 4:4 NASB

This means in every situation, especially during the uncomfortable pressures and situations of life. Paul was writing from firsthand experience—while he was in jail. Yet he did not allow his circumstances to imprison him in hopelessness and despair.

The revelation of the power and authority of joy, will come to your aid, and lift you above the fray, empowering you to fight *the good fight of faith.* The joy of the Lord, translates into supernatural strength, quickening your emotions and physical body. God has made you stronger than any enemy of grief and depression.

Winning Widows

And be not grieved and depressed; for the joy of the Lord is your strength and stronghold.
— Nehemiah 8:10 AMPC

If your present circumstances and feelings have robbed you of your joy, take heart my friends, you can get it back—start rejoicing! It may seem like a great effort because you are hurting, but make a quality decision to speak to *your feelings*, tell them to draw back. Open your mouth and start singing, rejoicing in the Lord. Your feelings will obey your command of faith and the supernatural strength of the Lord will rise up within you. The peace of God, which resides in your spirit is there for a purpose. This spiritual force keeps you calm and resolute even when the storm is raging, and the mountains look impossible. Your responsibility is to let His peace rule in your heart and mind. This peace passes all understanding; you can't work it out with your head.

The joy of the Lord is likened to oil, restoring healing and beauty into your life.

> *To proclaim the acceptable year of the Lord, and the day of vengeance of our God; to comfort all that mourn; To appoint unto them that mourn in Zion, to give unto them beautify for ashes, the oil of joy for mourning, the garment of praise for the spirit of heaviness; that they might be called trees*

Winning Widows

of righteousness, the planting of the Lord, that he might be glorified.   *– Isaiah 61:2 – 3*

Exchange mourning and sadness for the oil of joy and gladness. It washes over you, permeating your deepest emotions, infusing life and freedom into every step you take in faith along the journey to your destination. Don't set aside the ministry of the Holy Spirit in providing you with His joy and peace. Otherwise, the *spirit of heaviness* will quickly move in and drag you down. To be informed biblically is liberating, so much so that you will break forth into joyful laughter!

Joy and laughter work like medicine to your whole being, and brings healing to your physical body. Joy is spiritual warfare against weakness, sickness, and disease.

A merry heart doth good like a medicine; but a broken spirit drieth the bones.   *– Proverbs 17:22*

Father God, Our Way Maker

Thus saith the Lord, which maketh a way, and a path in the mighty water:...Behold, I will do a new thing: now it shall spring forth; shall ye not know it? I will even make a way in the wilderness, and rivers in the desert.   *– Isaiah 43:16, 19*

Winning Widows

Hope arises in the heart of the believer who takes God at His Word. Disappointments, can be like traveling through the desert, wandering and wondering what's next and asking yourself, "Will I ever come out of it?" This verse tells us exactly what God is up to! He is the way maker, whether it be through the water or through the desert or through grief. Nothing is impossible to our God and nothing is impossible to us who believe.

> *If thou canst believe, all things are possible to him that believeth.*   *– Mark 9:23*

Remember Naomi and Ruth as they set out to travel through the desert and rough terrain, to return to Bethlehem? Hope arose in their hearts, as they started on the faith adventure of a lifetime. They didn't stay in the desert, they moved forward to the destination called "blessings" that awaited them. God was about to do far above and beyond what they could imagine.

Our part is to DECLARE with our mouth what we believe in our heart, that God is making a beautiful way through the wilderness of disappointments and sadness. He is bringing us forth into a destination called— BLESSINGS. We must not talk out of DESPERATION but make faith-filled DECLARATIONS. Victorious end results belong to you, and are on the way!

Winning Widows
Alone But Not Alone

I've been a widow now for five years. My new life has not only been filled with challenges and changes, but an overwhelming sense of God's presence and loving care. I have a song in my heart and a shout of victory in my voice.

If you asked me, *"Are you ever lonely, Barbara?"* I would have to be honest and say, *"No, I am never lonely."* The peace and presence of the Lord is so real to me. That does not mean that I don't need the company of family and friends. I cherish my family and friends, and I keep closely connected to my Church family. I know it is not healthy emotionally or physically to withdraw and isolate myself from others. On the other hand, it is vitally important to spend time alone with God, and refresh your *spirit, soul,* and *body*; for, in God's presence, there is fullness of joy.

> *Thou wilt show me the path of life: in thy presence is fullness of joy; at thy right hand there are pleasures for evermore.* – Psalm 16:11

We are the Body of Christ: I need you in my life, and you need me. Each member of the Body of Christ is a particular member, meaning—we have *unique* gifts and distinctive attributes to *contribute* to each other. So make yourself available to be a blessing to others. And be will-

Winning Widows

ing to receive from those who desire to bless you too.

∼

The joy of the Lord translates into supernatural strength, quickening your emotions and physical body. God has made you stronger than any enemy of grief and depression.

To be real and down to Earth, there are and will be opportunities to feel lonely. As a believer, I know the antidote for loneliness is in God's Word, and great comfort is found in the sweet companionship of the Holy Spirit. Go to the Word of God and find Scriptures that promise you that God will never, never, ever leave you or forsake you. He is a present help—a now help, an ever-abiding help. Spending time daily worshiping the Lord and rejoicing in all His goodness, will lift you up. You will realize that you have been seated together with Jesus in the heavenly realm.

> *And hath raised us up together, and made us sit together in the heavenly places in Christ Jesus.*
> *– Ephesians 2:6*

You have access to the throne of God—to receive grace and help in time of need *(See: Hebrews 4:14 – 16)*. Jesus

Winning Widows

is the Friend that sticks to us closer than a brother.

> *I will not, I will not, I will not in any degree leave you helpless, nor forsake you, nor let you down (relax my hold on you), Assuredly no!*
> *— Hebrews 13:5 – 6 AMP*

Jesus is the Greater One, Who lives in your spirit, He is greater than loneliness. *(cf. 1 John 5:4)* He is far greater than fear. Practicing the presence of God by singing His praises and speaking His Word, will bring a real sense of His nearness to you.

I pray for each one of you today, that you will be filled with an inward knowing in your spirit of His abiding presence. You are NOT ALONE—NEVER!

Grace - An Unfair Advantage

Widows, there are numerous advantages to us who are now living in New Covenant realities. Naomi had a covenant with God under the Abrahamic blessing. This is what enabled her to experience restoration from her losses. Naomi's godly influence, prompted Ruth to follow her to the land of blessing. There she embraced the God of Abraham, Isaac, and Jacob.

Today, we have precious promises from God under

Winning Widows

our New Covenant, that can almost overwhelm us. We need a personal revelation of what belongs to us in Jesus. The truth is, God has already said 'Yes' and 'Amen' to His precious promises. *2 Corinthians 1:20* says, *For all the promises of God in him are yea, and in him Amen, unto the glory of God by us.*

Ask the Holy Spirit to bring an understanding and revelation to your heart and mind, that God really wants to manifest His gracious goodness to you. The Holy Spirit was given to teach us all things, including His grace, life and godliness. I pray you will embrace these precious and powerful words, causing your heart to rejoice and rise up in the life of God residing in your spirit. He is forever Faithful!

> *And I will pray the Father, and he shall give you another Comforter, that he may abide with you forever...But the Comforter, which is the Holy Ghost, whom the Father will send in my name, he shall teach you all things, and bring all things to your remembrance, whatsoever I have said unto you.*
> *– John 14:16, 26*

> *According as his divine power hath given us all things that pertain unto life and godliness, through the knowledge of him that hath called us to glory and virtue.* *– 1 Peter 1:3*

PRAYER CONFESSION FOR WINNING EVERY VICTORY IN LIFE:

Father God, because I am your child and in an unbreakable covenant with You through Jesus, and the blood of His cross, *I now reign in life* through the grace of God and the gift of righteousness. And because I reign in life, I proclaim my *liberty* and *freedom* from shame, grief and mourning. The Holy Spirit is my daily *Comforter*; He abides with me, teaches me, guides me, and brings revelation and counsel for every challenge I face in life. He is my strengthener, *advocate* and standby.

Lord, *You have given me beauty for ashes, and the oil of joy* instead of mourning. I put on my *garment of praise* each day, and the *spirit of heaviness* flees. For shame You have given me double and increased me and my family more and more.

The joy of the Lord is my strength. I choose to magnify you, Lord, for your marvelous goodness and mercy to me. *I am more than a conqueror through Him that loved me* with an everlasting love. You never leave me or forsake me

Lord, You are my rewarder and giver of *every good and perfect gift*. My hope and faith is in You! I cannot be defeated because *You always cause me to triumph!* Praise the Lord!

ABOUT THE AUTHOR

(Continued from back cover) ...

For over fifty years she and her husband Gordon traveled and ministered together on six continents. Their anointed husband and wife ministry began in the United Kingdom, followed by pastoral ministry in the United States. From 1988 they flowed in the prophet's anointing to the nations. Throughout their pastoral and international ministry, the Lord was pleased to confirm His Word through many signs and wonders. By the anointing of the Holy Spirit, miracles, healing gifts and prophetic utterances have followed the preaching and teaching of God's Word.

Barbara's loving husband, Gordon White, was promoted to Heaven on June 26, 2014. She continues to follow God's plan for her life, teaching faith, healing, and motivating the body of Christ to live in victory. Her ministry flows in the anointing with manifestations of the gifts of the Holy Spirit.

Barbara believes and continually shares that The Gospel is GOOD NEWS! Freedom from sin is GOOD NEWS! Freedom from the curse is GOOD NEWS. Healing, health, and prosperity are GOOD NEWS! Knowing you can live a victorious and holy life because you have been made the righteousness of God in Christ is GOOD NEWS!

ABOUT THE AUTHOR

Live in the light of the knowledge of the goodness of God. Let Him bless you today and everyday!

Her book *"Navigating Through The Maze of Grief"*, is an anointed book that is helping many heal from the pain of loss and grief.

Books available by the Author on Amazon.com
- **Navigating Through The Maze of Grief**
- **Say The Word**
- **Our Love Journey:** A Memoir of Gordon & Barbara White's Life and International Ministry spanning over fifty years
- **Job's Jeopardy"** A Study in the book of Job

BARBARA'S RESOURCES

Winning Widows is a group page on Facebook, devoted to ministering to the emotional support and spiritual needs of widows, and those who have lost loved ones. You are invited to join this page to receive daily inspirational Bible devotions.

Faith Ministries International: Barbara's ministry page is available on Facebook. When you join, you will receive monthly teaching newsletters and ministry updates.

ABOUT THE AUTHOR

Barbara is available to speak to your church, group, or teaching seminar.

www.fmint.org

Enjoy these other great books from Bold Truth Publishing

Seemed Good to THE HOLY GHOST
by Daryl P Holloman

Effective Prison Ministries
by Wayne W. Sanders

TURN OFF THE STEW
by Judy Spencer

The Holy Spirit SPEAKS Expressly
by Elizabeth Pruitt Sloan

Matthew 4:4
Man shall not live by bread alone...
by Rick McKnight

VICTIM TO VICTOR (THE CHOICE IS YOURS)
by Rachel V. Jeffries

SPIRITUAL BIRTHING
Bringing God's Plans & Purposes and Manifestation
by Lynn Whitlock Jones

BECOMING PERFECT
Let The Perfector Perfect His Work In You
by Sally Stokes Weiesnbach

FIVE SMOOTH STONES
by Aaron Jones

Available at select bookstores and
www.BoldTruthPublishing.com

The story of a dynamic husband and wife team, likened to a modern day Aquila and Priscilla.

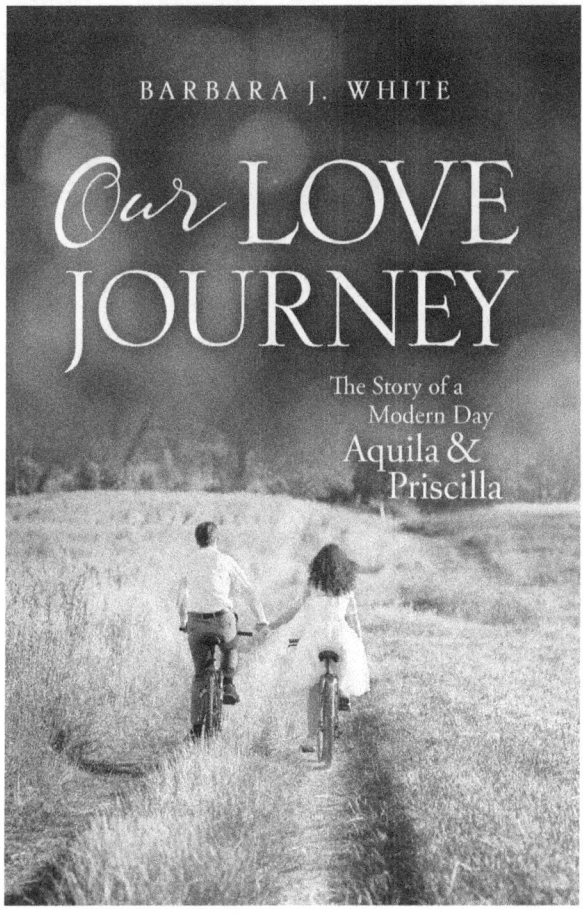

This love story is amazing and unique. It is a beautiful journey Gordon and Barbara White shared together for fifty years; ministering to the nations on six continents. Filled with bold testimonies of healings and God's miracle working power; this true story will motivate you to follow God's plan for your life.

Available through this ministry, select bookstores, and Amazon.com

**Why do we confess the Word of God?
Did Jesus confess the Word of God?**

If you have been dismayed when trouble or crisis come your way, then *SAY THE WORD* will help you to understand the importance of saying what God says in His Word.

Available through this ministry, select bookstores, and Amazon.com

In this book, the Author explores: what's on the other side of a death—for those of us still living?

- Surviving the loss of a loved one.
- Avoiding the grip of grief.
- Defeating loneliness and fear.
- How to face the future.

You are not alone as you walk through your maze of grief; there is a place called "the other side" waiting for you. It is a beautiful life of victory and joy.

Available through this ministry, select bookstores, and Amazon.com

Evangelist and Teacher *Barbara J. White* tackles some of the fallacies, misunderstandings and erroneous doctrines concerning the oldest writing in the Bible; the Book of Job.

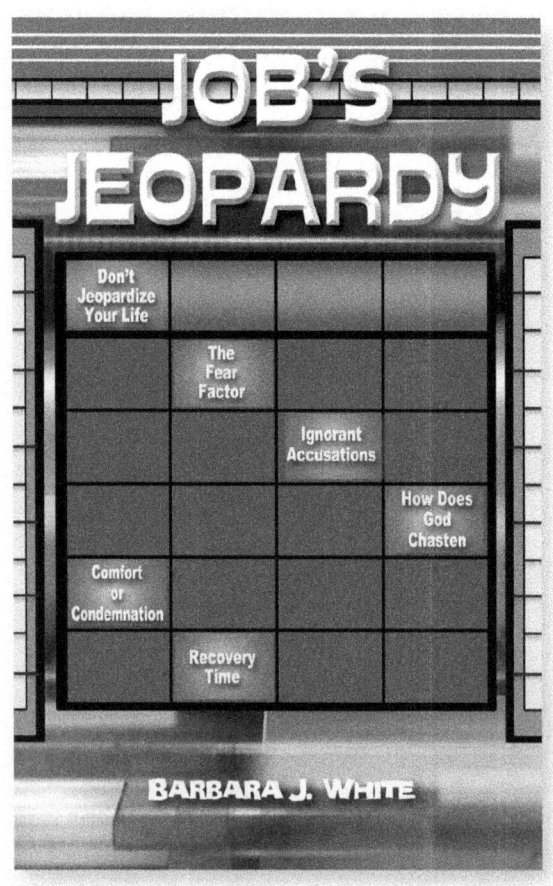

Get the whole picture, get the true picture—let's set this record straight! JOB'S JEOPARDY is an intregal study tool for Sunday Schools, Bible and Word Studies, Seminaries, or a great addition to any Faith Library.

Available through this ministry, select bookstores, and Amazon.com

www.ingramcontent.com/pod-product-compliance
Lightning Source LLC
Chambersburg PA
CBHW070655050426
42451CB00008B/359